You Can't Play With Us!

The Adventures of Bam & Jam

For more information, address: info@rdclarkson.co.uk

FIRST EDITION

www.rdclarkson.co.uk

For my family

&

For Blu and Mya my Alaskan Malamutes,
without whom there would be no story.

Bam was just waking from his nap. He could hear Jam playing.

I wonder what's going on, he thought.

So up he got.

He stretched and let out a big yawn. Now he was ready to see what all the fuss was about.

Mum and Dad were holding a collar and lead each.
Bam and Jam knew exactly what that meant...
"Walkies!" Mum shouted.

Their paws began to dance and they barked impatiently.
Bam and Jam wiggled with excitement.

Once they had their collars and leads on, they pulled Mum and Dad out to the car.

Bam and Jam spent the whole journey to the park with their noses pressed against the window, eager to get out and play.

When they arrived, they jumped out of the car as soon as the boot was open.

They sat on the grass and waited to be unclipped from their leads.

Then off they went, chasing one another and barking happily.

Under the watchful eyes of Mum and Dad, Bam and Jam played for a few more minutes.
Until they spotted something across the park.

More dogs! Before they ran over, they looked at Mum and Dad with their big, brown eyes.

"Can we play? Please please please!" they asked.

"Go and see!" Mum and Dad said.

The other dogs were all playing together, chasing each other, wrestling and fetching sticks.

But as soon as Bam and Jam arrived, they stopped and stared at them.

The other dogs didn't look happy.

A small, ginger dog with wiry curls barked at Bam.

"You can't play with us.
You're too big!"

"And I don't like your ears." Growled a big, skinny grey dog to Jam.

Jam hid behind Bam.

Bam wiggled his bum and howled excitedly. "We only want to play!"

“Go play somewhere else, we don’t like dogs like you.” Snapped a different dog, with brown patches and long floppy ears.

Bam's tail stopped wagging and he stood up straight. "Fine!" he barked back at them, loudly.

The other owners all rushed over to collect their dogs when they heard Bam's bark.
They even shouted at Mum and Dad too.

Jam sat on Dad's feet and leant against him.

"It's ok, don't be sad," Dad said. "Some dogs aren't taught that even though we're all different, we can still be friends."

Bam squeezed between Mum's legs, like he used to do when he was a puppy.

"It's not your fault," Mum said.

Bam and Jam walked slowly back towards the car, they wanted to go home now.

Their tails weren't wagging anymore.

Everyone was sad. They had only wanted to play.

They saw another group of dogs playing and chasing each other, but Bam and Jam just kept walking.
They probably wouldn't want to play either, they thought.

All of a sudden, a tiny dog raced in front of them. She stopped and dropped her ball.

"Wow! Look how *BIG* you are!"

But Bam and Jam were still sad, so they just kept walking.

The tiny dog barked and wagged her little tail.

Then a second dog ran over to them. He had silky black fur and a friendly face.

"Your fur is so *SOFT!* It's like a cloud!"

Bam and Jam looked at each other, confused. They weren't used to other dogs being so nice to them.

A third dog came running over. It skidded to a halt right in front of them both.

"Hey! Your ears are just like mine, and you're fluffy like me too!"

The third dog was smaller than Bam and Jam, but bigger than the other two. She wagged her tail and wiggled her bum in the air, wanting to play.

The tiny dog rolled the ball to Bam. All three of the new dogs danced excitedly.

"You really want to play with us?" Jam asked.

"YES!"

Bam's tail began to wag. He crouched down low, scooped the ball up in his mouth and *ZOOM!* Off he went!

Jam howled playfully.

The dogs chased each other and rolled around on the grass in a big mess of tails, legs and fluff.

Bam and Jam were so happy.

Mum and Dad were happy too. They always knew that Bam and Jam would make friends that like them just the way they are.

Lightning Source UK Ltd.
Milton Keynes UK
UKHW051020090721
386882UK00005B/123

9 781527 292789